The Mother Myths

by Zoë Etkin

motherhood pages

writings and wisdom for mothers by mothers

www.motherhoodpages.com

Copyright © 2022 by Zoë Etkin

Motherhood Pages has the exclusive rights to reproduce this work, to prepare derivative works from this work, to publicly distribute this work, to publicly perform this work, and to publicly display this work.

All rights reserved. No part of this publication may be reproduced, stored in a retrieval system, or transmitted, in any form or by any means, electronic, mechanical, photocopying, recording, or otherwise, without the prior written permission of the copyright owner.

Printed in the United States of America
ISBN 978-0-578-35825-3

I dedicate this book to my daughter, June Margaret, who made me a mother, to my own mother, and to all the mothers I have cared for over the last decade.

TABLE OF CONTENTS

Mythography 1
    "We are fed the Mother Myths…" 3

Natal 5
    "Mix the blood…" 7
    "The glowing confession…" 8
    "I do not know this body…" 9
    "From the moment…" 10
    "You are of the water…" 11
    "Who am I now…" 12
    "They're there, soft…" 13
    "Creating life is…" 14
    "I hate these…" 15
    "The myth of the line…" 17
    "There's milk and…" 18
    "I tick the box…" 19
    "We must…" 20
    "I've lost it…" 21
    "They don't tell you…" 22
    "Don't cry, he says…" 23
    "And where…" 25
    "I didn't walk…" 26

Untethered 29
    "This is for you…" 31
    "I need more time in the dark…" 32
    "The story of…" 33
    "It seems to be…" 35
    "The dark of me…" 36
    "The myth of the body…" 37
    "Is it the myth…" 39
    "The ocean in me…" 40
    "No one tells you…" 41
    "I live for your quiet…" 42
    "The love a mother has…" 44
    "Is there science behind…" 45

Seen 47
    "This has made me..." 49
    "When will we..." 50
    "The myth of sex..." 51
    "I know I deserve..." 53
    "I wish I had..." 54
    "I look for an ending..." 55
    "No wonder they said..." 56
    "We learn to stay..." 57
    "At bedtime..." 59
    "I grieve that I will..." 60
    "I need to get better..." 61
    "The myth of joy..." 62
    "I'm different now..." 64
    "The light can touch..." 65

Mythopoeia 67
    "I cast my own..." 69

MYTHOGRAPHY

We are fed the Mother Myths our whole girlhood. To give is to love. To love is our deepest joy. There is no Mother's body—it is not hers to own. There is no grief or loss—make more, start again. The Mother does not desire—the Mother is satisfied. The Mother's pleasure is in her children and in care of the home. The Mother doesn't rage—she never yells, she never breaks. We pass them down, mother to daughter, in baby dolls, doll houses, and playing house. But you see, now I am there. I am Mother. Mythic. Tearing into myself. Holding out my hands and showing her the guts of the thing. Letting her see behind the curtain to what has always been. It hurts to expose her to the ugliness of it, but I must, for her Mothering, should she choose it, will be a reckoning.

*

NATAL

Mix the blood

with earth

Make me the Holy Mother

Build a shrine

to flat breasts wide across

full bellies

full hips

full thighs

*

The glowing confession

of my out of control joy/grief

as I incubate the ravenous

babe

I am nerve-heavy

bloated

I'm a mirrored

apology

I chose this

remember?

(Or so he reminds)

What more

can I

ask for?

*

I do not know this body

this brain

this spirit

                    *

From the moment

you entered me

I felt your

your light

and I grew in

its shadow

*

You are of the water

the Bearer

like my own mother

You are the flow

and I the riverbank

holding and bending

to you

You are of the water

and you bubble up

into my throat

each morning

You are the flow

an immaculate ripple

in my belly

*

Who am I now

that you

are manifested

in flesh

Who am I now

that I live

to hold you

oxygenate you

embody

you

*

They're there, soft, before she's born. But the morbid thoughts begin their placid cascade once I see her perfect little body for the first time. There's been a fly trapped in the house for days, now conducting its dying song upon a lightbulb, distracting me from the earliest memory of my daughter's face. In that first viewing, I was struck with the realization that I will never get to see her when she is old. That I've made this beautiful person and I don't get to experience the entirety of her life. That there will be a foreseeable end to this.

*

Creating life is
creating
death

*

I hate these

short dark

days of

unyielding winter

Postpartum

(postmortem)

body (self)

in various states of

decay

My life force

escaping out of

every pore

every orifice

All the pads

soaking me up

Little fish mouth

eating me up

There's a long

night ahead

met by a cold

morning

My breath

hangs in the air

cumulous

There would

be a black sky

above

if not for

the pollutive

glow of the city—

behemoth

metropolis

of isolation

*

The myth of the line
that it goes on
endless

       *

There's milk and a sweet smell. The bed sheets, mangled. The bed is gravity—I slink toward it, whether I want to or not. I live in a body I do not know. A lot of people never bounce back. I went through a big thing but no one wants to hear about it. It's too hot and I'm not used to feeling my breasts against my ribcage. This is my life right now—this mattress, this dark room. Looking back on the birth, how it didn't happen here. Some nights I've sat awake, watching them sleep, scratching blood all over the sheets. We do this, women, and we become wild. The bottom of the ocean—that's a place I've been. I pull the cool sand up over me like a blanket. A little fish swims alongside, asleep, but on the move. It's hard to rest next to the squirm. The first time I felt her was alarming. Tiny thing. Perpetual thing. She was awake in me. Now I wake for her. I breathe for her. We aren't alone. There are other eyes. Other hungry mouths. She and I are made of the same sand; therefore, I must allow her to slip through my fingers. She becomes her own, and I become my own again.

*

I tick the box for today: I was good. Didn't rage, didn't threaten to leave. Made a nice dinner for the family. Vacuumed the rug and dusted. Today, I didn't feel like hurting anyone, not even myself. I took the dog on her walks and put the baby to bed without trouble. Still, I've lost the ability to sit with myself. Who am I without her? Raw pile of flesh, open wound of a psyche. I walked the line between identities. Grew my belly out to here. Endured the petting and fawning that comes with it. I didn't know what I was feeling. I didn't know that no amount of love could take away a pain so primal. Maybe it is our curse: to bleed and bear. To leak milk and weep centuries of female tears. I can't promise I'll be good tomorrow. I tell myself to be, but the savage grief written on my bones is older than trees, older than air.

*

We must

never forget

we are

animals

*

I've lost it. All of it. The view from here is diffuse, a bit muddied like a blind painter's last canvas. Hard to breathe too. Bricks on my chest. When I brought myself here, I thought I knew something. Now, seven years later, I find I'm child-minded again. A few nights ago I held a pair of nail scissors to my wrist but drew no blood. What is it to be brave? I want to not be here, in the general sense, but then I imagine the fallout, and that isn't good either. I tell him I'll stay. Take off my shoes, my purse falling to the floor in a thud. There's only so many times I can threaten it, or even come close to doing it, before something has to change. This view, from right here where my feet meet the dirt, it's what I have for today. It's what I make myself about. These thin clouds, the gray hanging over the freeway. I can construct a person with this view, a personality. The palms, the purple jacaranda, the black crows ripping at trash: they become me. The guy standing on the median with a guitar and tinny amp: me. The gulls, the ocean: I take them in. I don't know why it works, but these pieces of city begin to mend me. In time, the view shifts from dull gray to crisp blue. This happens when the winds move through the valley. Then the black night, the stars and all. My feet still in contact with the earth.

*

They don't tell you

that after you have

a baby

you have to learn

how to be a person

again

*

"Don't cry," he says. "Keep it together for her. We have to be strong for her." I can't be strong anymore. I spent all my strong in labor, in pushing her out as fast as I could. And who is he to tell me to keep myself together when I see the string unraveling at his edges? Let me succumb to having nothing left to give. Stop censoring me. I might have bound my belly but that doesn't mean I am healed. I'm having a hard time understanding how a postpartum, lactating body goes back to work. My body needs her, yet I am desperate for my arms to be empty. I feel pulled apart, further widened away from myself. I read somewhere, "We are not a species designed to cope alone." Then why, Myth Mother, must you have it all? Why teach us to be everything for everyone and nothing for ourselves? He is here but he isn't enough. I take it all on so he doesn't have to. But he wants to. I push him away from her because I don't trust that he will sacrifice himself in the way that I do. As if this thinned version of me is what she needs. He isn't enough. I'm not enough. Grandmother isn't enough. Doula isn't enough. We are owed more. We are designed for more. I want someone to blame who isn't me. I need someone to take this child and let me rest. Deep, thick sleep that I know will never come again. Here I am: not alone and still not coping. He is right here in this bed, snoring in spite of my suffering, my engorgement, my crawling skin. This old narrative keeps being written. We allow it, we reinforce it. We send little daddies off to work while little mommies tend to baby and put on their apron before presenting a beautiful wooden dinner to the daddies when they return after a hard day of building toy skyscrapers.

*

And where

are fathers

made

What language

is passed down

through blood

and fists

to little boys

Who teaches

them distance

Who builds

these men

so fragile

*

I didn't walk

blindly

into the befogged

chasm

In fact

I

hurtled myself

down at breakneck

speed

knowing it would

hurt

knowing it would

steal me of

my youth

And yet

not knowing

what love

I would

find

there

*

UNTETHERED

This is for you

and it isn't

My life is about you

and it isn't

There are many

heart beats

many hands

ever present

around me

When will I be

singular?

Perhaps

never

perhaps

never

*

I need more time in the dark
to think about the light
I'm not living in

                        *

The story of

a mother's love

is that it's

limitless

implicit

The first

love we know

and the last

love we

cry out for

But I know

mothers

and the love I see

is deep in the bones

wavers between

firm and yielding

can be fractured

is holy and

imperfect

*

It seems to be

my job

to share this

dark gospel

It's me

who keeps

splashing light

everywhere

Me bringing

deathtalks

to the pretty painted

nurseries

But I see myself

in their eyes

I see what we all crave—

a shred of

the truth

*

The dark of me is strong. Thoughts of death drop down into me, but from where? My mother? Her mother? How far back in the lineage were we taught to hide the soft of our selves? I will suck it out like poison. I will alchemize it, or more likely let it dismantle me. My body. My marriage. Don't think I'm not trying. I am tending to what can be tended. I give myself this room to be silent in. Even the fly has quieted. He gently traverses the ceiling joists. Soon he'll starve and I'll find him, belly up on the floor, surrounded by dust and hair. The black of him against the pale oak. I'll leave him there until he crumbles. A dry shell. A thing I cannot tend to.

*

The myth of the body

is that it goes back

but we all know

it never does

The body

has its own

temporal law

is always

living in the past

present and future

writing our

darkest secrets

onto the smallest parts

of our cells

The body reminds

the body insists

the body begs to be

seen

And some of us

begin to shout—

stop hiding it

stop hiding it

                        *

Is it the myth

telling me I want

another baby?

Or is it the ancient brain

residing at the base

of my skull?

It's not my mother

this time

I pack my

ears with cotton

to damper

the call

of the spiritbaby

*

The ocean in me swells with a warning: *It's the salt that alters fresh water to brine.* (His salt). I once grew a blooming reef and sheltered a tiny, silvery fish 'til she was ready to slip through the coral archway. She took the reef with her. *It's okay,* I tell myself. *I like feeling still.* Too much salt kills. Even the Dead Sea is dying.

*

No one tells you

becoming a mother

changes your relationship

with time

That it will move like molasses

or barrel ahead

That it will cave in on itself

and pull you backwards

to your very own reflection

of who you once were

All in one day

*

I live for your quiet

sleeping face

that I have watched

nearly every night

since I pulled you

out of me

Four years

I have comforted

you into sleep

with my breasts

my arms

Your chest

on my chest

our breath

the same

rise and fall

syncing and sinking

into sleep

*

The love

a mother has

with her child

is vulnerable

In no other relationship

will someone know you

from the guts

In no other love

will they touch the ugliness

of you and

still call it

home

*

Is there science behind

the amnesia

that begins to set in

mere hours

after you

open your pelvis

or abdomen

to give forth

to the world

the next

human animal?

I need to see

it quantified

and peer reviewed

so I can

create

the counter agent

and restore

our collective

remembering

                                        *

SEEN

This has made me intolerant. This has taken what little I had for you and given it all to her, to the house, to my career, to the animals I wish we never adopted. I don't know where to stand. To my right, the rock; to my left, the hard place. Neither looks appealing, nor livable. It's not just the Myth Mother whispering for me to "stay together for the kids," but the Holy Wife, the one who has it all and gives and gives without falter, without fatigue. She's the picture of a mid-century housewife humming "Stand by Your Man," as she vacuums in pearls and takes a boring fuck in a twin bed next to another twin bed. I wouldn't mind that set up with you. Just enough distance to feel free. *Sometimes it's hard to be a woman*, croons the Wife, *giving all your love to just one man*. Who is he, I wonder? This man who earns her arms to cling to, her bed to stand by in the middle of the night with a beaming erection? Maybe I've just never met him. Or I'm queer. Non-monogamous? Aberrant? I can't see the arc of my story unfolding ahead of me. Here, in the hopeless present, I see brick, I see granite.

*

When will we

stop trying to

love men

who don't

love themselves?

We keep naming

our souls and

bodies to them

keep giving them

fatherhood

and expecting

them to understand

what it's like for

the heart to drop down

through one's body

and walk around

on two legs

*

The myth of sex

that he'll want it

always

(ever)

That as a mother

it's not about

my desire

But I received

no coaching

regarding his lack

We're always

wanting too much

or not enough

Six weeks

or four years—

the distance

from birth doesn't

matter anymore

Scars still ache

but the need

to be taken

holds firm

The bloom

between

my legs

is finally

open

and I ask him

Are you ready?

*

I know I deserve

better than to

live in his

darkness

but what's more

is how I worry

what it's doing

to you

and your precious

light

*

I wish I had

the strength

to be the mother

you deserve

*

I look for an

ending

but don't

find the

right words

There's no tidy

way to pull the pieces

of him

out of

me

(and do I

want to?)

*

No wonder they said the womb would wander the body; she is lonely. She weeps and I catch it all. I'm red all over and I wander the rooms of our house looking for him: bedridden, vacillating between two poles. I forget how magnets work, but I know two negatives repel, fling each other away. He's right here. I'm right here. We mirror each other in the bed like students in an acting class, sensing and moving, reflexively. Sometimes my fingers might seek out the edge of his body, but his sleep brain manically guards. He remains untouched. And later, when the child wanders in at dusk, I am the chosen body to cling to.

*

We learn to

stay

when we shouldn't

We choose

comfort

over happiness

We realize

we will never be

free

Always tethered

always entwined

by our children

through no fault

of their own

They didn't

choose

this life

We summoned them

and now we must decide

how to divvy them up

should we have the gall

to leave

                     *

At bedtime, he makes a fuss about the windows. That I haven't drawn the curtains. From the moment he brought home the screaming child, I've gathered up every tiresome ounce of patience left in me to hear her, to help her pee, to affirm her frustration at having to wear a diaper to bed, to wrestle her into footed pajamas. Now, I hold and calm her and usher her to sleep and he says it's nothing. The windows. The windows! How I could smash them to pieces if not for the noise.

*

I grieve that I will

(that I should only)

mother once

Because I do long

for more children

But you must know

that you are enough

and with only you

I have the space I need

to find myself

And, in doing so

be better for you

*

I need to get

better

at appreciating

my ability to do

so much

in the face of

so much

*

The myth of joy

how we're robbed

of it

how we're judged

when we can't

find it

How we long for it

getting glimpses

when our baby smiles

or we wake without pain

or we stumble upon some

hiding amongst

dead leaves

in the wintering yard

Should I search for it

inside myself?

If so, where should I look?

The heart muscle?

The brain matter?

It's in the movement

of the dura

The spine unwinds

with joy

                *

I'm different now

in the world

More comfortable

with living

in this body

I can't say

I have lost the fear

of death

But under

every step

the rhizomatic

network

connects me

to something

older and deeper

than us all

*

The light can

touch

all the places

where I was hurt

and now have

healed

I am ready to be

seen

*

MYTHOPOEIA

I cast my own mythology. Pomegranate. Underworld. Moon. Tide. Labyrinth. Hero. Daughter. Milk. Cave. Soil. Bone. Clay. I draw lines down each arm in coal, extending onto the ground before me. Ritual becomes a way to mother—myself, my child, the women I serve. We need re-mothering, re-birthing, re-mythologizing from that which was spoon fed to us from infancy forward. I pour a salt circle around me for protection. No one held me when I needed to be held. Where did they go? They promised they wouldn't leave me. I place three stones in the center of the circle. The Maiden. The Mother. The Crone. I'm less interested in the little deaths between each archetype and more in how they layer. I set the stones on top of one another. A multiverse. I let go of individual states of being. Everything builds upon the thing before and the thing before forever exists, even if dormant, even if dead. Maybe I died when I gave birth, but I'm still a here. I'm still something. Turning over the earth for new growth, then ripping life from the soil, as we're taught. What comes next is usually fire, or water, or wind. I sit still in the circle with my eyes closed and wait for an answer. Who is needed to complete this act? I could watch it all burn—the flame entices and draws me in. Or get swept up in a flood. The wind is a centrifuge—no, mustn't disperse the layers. The baby years have come and gone, my bones have moved closer to one another again, my love for you is painfully expansive, but my nerves are shot. It's earth, always earth. On hands and knees, I rock and shudder, and speak with clear voice: I am a mother.

I am a woman. I am a body. I deserve pleasure. I deserve rest. I deserve sex. I create. I destroy. I love. I bleed. I scream. I scream. I matter I matter I matter I fucking matter.

*

www.ingramcontent.com/pod-product-compliance
Lightning Source LLC
Chambersburg PA
CBHW072019290426
44109CB00018B/2290